DATE DUE

APR 15 1999	
FEB 17 2000	
MAR 17 2000	
AUG 26 2002	
APR 09 DA	

BRODART, CO.   Cat. No. 23-221-003

Secrets of Flowers

Secrets of Flowers

as revealed by A. Stoddard Kull

Illustrated by Arthur W. Schmidt

The Stephen Greene Press

Brattleboro, Vermont

This book has been produced
in the United States of America:
designed by R. L. Dothard Associates,
composed by American Book–Stratford Press,
and printed and bound by The Colonial Press.

It is published by The Stephen Greene Press,
Brattleboro, Vermont 05301

LIBRARY OF CONGRESS CATALOGING IN PUBLICATION DATA

Kull, A. Stoddard.
  Secrets of flowers.

  1. Flowers (in religion, folk-lore, etc.)
2. Flower language. I. Schmidt, Arthur W.
II. Title.
GR780.K84   1976   398'.368'213   75–41875
ISBN 0–8289–0269–0

Contents

Preface

ITHIN these pages you may find, as you have been promised, Secrets of Flowers. Not all the secrets, by any means; for flowers have disclosed such a multitude of facts and portents, omens and implications, legends and properties, that we can but set forth several of the most diverting; and doubtless, to be sure, our Flora as yet keep some of the very best secrets to themselves. The Referencers in the back of this book indicate the sentiments expressed by a hundred flowers, and the flowers which reveal a hundred sentiments. There are, in addition, fifty-two flowers presented in detail, of whose secrets we have been privileged to hear tell on occasion: a modest but not insubstantial number. You may liken it to the number of weeks in a year, in each of which some secrets may be proved and practiced; though we rather incline to favor its likeness to the number of cards in a deck, containing in their variety an infinity of combinations and designs, of *secrets* to be sure, emerging only under the spell of a wise and guiding hand. Such a hand was that of John Gerard, master of the flower knowledge; and with him we may ask truly,

Who would look dangerously up at Planets
that might safely look downe at Plants?

A. S. K.

CLOVER
Think of me

Clover

THE HUMBLE Clover has long been esteemed as a valuable defense against snakes and evil spirits; and many a peasant who found it necessary to cross a dark field by night has plucked a Clover leaf to guard against intimidations by fairies and sprites. The Clover came into its present renown through its service to St. Patrick, who used it while he was converting Ireland to demonstrate the unity of the Trinity to his listeners. The Irish were the more ready to accept the Clover as a beneficent omen, feeling as they did that it symbolized the national virtues of Love, Heroism, and Wit.

All authorities are agreed on the lucky properties of a four-leafed Clover; yet while some maintain that a five-leafed Clover is lucky to give away, others tell us that such Clover should be avoided entirely.

If powdered Lime be thrown upon bare soil, there may spring up a crop of white Clover where it has never grown before. This is an infallible indication of fertile and promising soil.

The possessor of a four-leafed Clover is proof against any witchcraft which may be attempted against him; and if a maiden place such a clover in her left shoe, the first man she meets, or his brother, will become her husband.

To dream of a field of Clover is one of the most fortuitous auguries known, foretelling prosperity and health, and success to the lover.

3

Heliotrope

DEVOTION

THE NAME Heliotrope signifies a plant which turns toward the sun; and Virgil tells us a very pretty story about a maiden, lost for love of Apollo, who reclined along the ground, ever searching the heavens for a sight of her beloved. In fact, it is apparent that Virgil's Heliotrope was quite a different flower from ours: and for our modest purple flower we shall have to create a new legend or else do without.

The uses to which the Heliotrope may be put are described succinctly by Albertus Magnus: "Gather in August the Heliotropon, wrap it in a Bay-leaf with a wolf's tooth, and it will, if placed under the pillow, show a man who has been robbed where are his goods, and who has taken them. Also, if placed in a church, it will keep fixed in their places all the women present who have broken their marriage vows. This last is most tried and most true."

The Heliotrope is a native of the mountains of Peru, where it came under the influence of Leo. This is the reason for this flower's extraordinary sympathy for the month of August. If the Heliotrope be picked in this month, and used to do some evil, that evil will return upon the wrong-doer.

4

DAISY

Innocence

Daisy

HE Daisy is on the whole the favorite flower of all British poets. Spenser, for one, speaks kindly of

The little daizie that at evening closes.

A well-known practice of maids who have lost their hearts, wishing to determine whether they are ever to receive recompense, is to pluck one by one the petals from the Daisy, chanting, "He loves me—loves me not," the while. The last petal and the last phrase determine the situation.

The Daisy is the flower of the "Maid Marguerite, meek and mild" of Antioch, whose prayers for women about to become mothers saved many lives and enshrined her in their love.

Spring has not arrived until you can set your foot on twelve Daisies.

To dream of Daisies in Springtime or Summer is a lucky omen; but to dream of them in Fall or Winter portends ill.

In Thuringia, upon the extraction of a tooth, a person must eat three Daisies to be henceforth free from toothache.

King Henry the Eighth consumed many Daisies in a futile effort to rid himself of ulcers.

Jasmine
GRACE

HEN, in 1699, a Jasmine plant was procured from Goa by the Grand Duke of Tuscany, he was so jealous of the flower of which he owned the only example that he forbade his gardener to give a cutting to anyone. The gardener, however, was just then in love. On the birthday of his betrothed, he gave her a bouquet containing a single Jasmine flower. The girl took pains to grow more such flowers; following the gardener's instructions, she sold cuttings from the plant and became rich. The happy couple was soon married; and the damsels of Tuscany still wear a Jasmine wreath on their wedding days.

On Crucifixion night, when other flowers died of sorrow, the Jasmine folded its flowers; it was never to show color again. That is why the Jasmine, once a bright pink, now shows only the palest hues.

Shenstone's beloved Phillis must have been lovely indeed, since he represents her—

More Fair, and
More sweet than the jessamine flower

To dream of Jasmine means the highest good fortune. It is most particularly a favorable portent for lovers, as it signifies early marriage.

TULIP
Declaration of love

Tulip

UR IDEA of the significance of the Tulip seems to derive from the Persians. Among those people, the Tulip is the floral offering made by a young man to his beloved. By this he says, "as the redness of this flower, I am' on fire with love" and "as the blackness of its center, my heart is burnt to a coal."

The love that some men have for flowers might truly be said to be a passion; yet it is seldom so evident as was the case in Holland, during the "Tulip Madness" of the seventeenth century. Then was the appreciation of the Tulip brought to such a pitch, or frenzy, that respected men of fortune might spend thousands upon thousands for the bulb of an original species.

The once-fierce Turks show perhaps their more modest nature in their annual celebration of the flower, the Feast of the Tulips. At these festivities the leaves of the Tulip are devoured, following which the Turkish men and maidens disport themselves in Oriental fashion.

The Tulip is apparently much a flower of the East; and indeed one of its most playful encomiums has been given it by the Persian poet Hafez, who pondered, "Perhaps the tulip feared the evils of destiny; thence while it lives, it bears the wine goblet on its stalk."

Lilac

FIRST EMOTIONS OF LOVE

THOUGH the beauty and fragrance of the Lilac make it one of our most beloved garden flowers, it was but charily that the Lilac was admitted indoors, its purple hues denoting mourning and sadness to many. Indeed, it has been said that she who wears Lilacs will never wear a wedding ring; and in more modest days than ours, one commonly sent a bouquet of Lilacs to a young lady with whom one wished to break off an engagement.

The origin of the White Lilac is of related interest. An English nobleman ruined a trusting maiden and caused her death of a broken heart. Overcome with remorse, he caused a clump of Lilacs to be planted on her grave; and those who saw them said that these flowers were white in the morning just before sunrise.

To find a Lilac blossom with five instead of four corolla lobes means good luck.

M. Proust, the decadent French novelist, was able even in his cork-lined room to evoke "l'odeur d'invisibles et persistants lilas."

GENTIAN
Loveliness

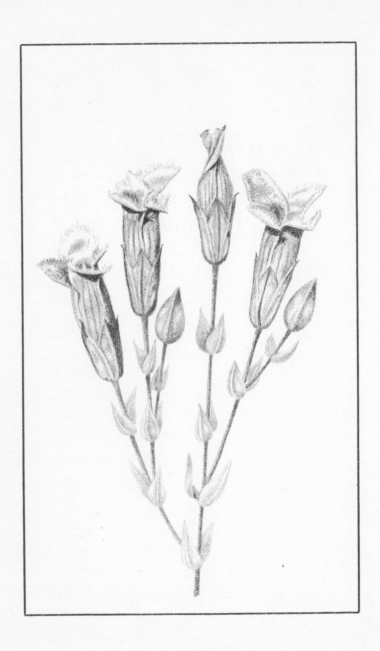

Gentian

THE GENTIAN has long been revered for its medicinal powers. Physicians of old believed the flower to be "sovrayne" over poisons, pestilences, indigestions, dog bites, stubborn livers, lameness, and other maladies. It bears the name of Gentius, King of Illyria, who discovered its healing properties.

Ladislas, beloved King of Hungary, found in the Gentian relief from a plague which beset his country. He went into the fields bearing his bow and arrow, and prayed that his shaft be directed to some plant which might stem the ravages of the disease. He shot, and the arrow flew to the root of a Gentian, which the King took up, and with which wondrous cures were wrought.

The Fringed Gentian, close relation of the Gentian, was celebrated by the American poet, William Cullen Bryant, in these lines:

> Thou waitest late, and com'st alone,
> When woods are bare and birds are flown,
> And frosts and shortening days portend
> The aged year is near an end.

Mimosa
SENSITIVENESS

HE DELICATE Mimosa is commonly known as the "Sensitive plant," and its peculiar activities are familiar to us all. One need but touch its leaf, however gently, and this modest plant retracts its foliage immediately to shield itself from further contact. It may seem to some that it were to be modest to a fault, to be so very retiring; and hardier spirits than the Mimosa have called it the emblem of Prudery. But it is with flowers as it is with maidens, *De indolibus non disputandum.*

Our remarking upon the Mimosa in connection with maidenly virtue has full precedent among the ancients; for this plant was born of just such a consideration. The Greek maid Cephisa inspired Pan with a violent passion, so that she had to flee from him in terror. The satyr caught her, but her appeal to the gods was answered, and she was transformed for her protection into the Mimosa.

It was, further, an old belief that if a girl passed by this plant in a state of sin, it would recoil as if touched by an evil hand.

The Indian Mimosa tree has many magical properties, and a sprig of its leaves are a complete protection against wicked spells and the Evil Eye.

16

ROSE
Love

Rose

THE ORIGIN of the red Rose has been variously explained. The ancients believed it to have been stained by Venus' blood, when her fingers were wounded by its thorns. Herrick gives a more cheerful explanation, that

> As Cupid danced among
> The Gods, he down the nectar flung;
> Which on the white Rose being shed,
> Made it, forever after, red.

The Rose is a symbol of fidelity, as well as an expression of beauty: it is said that the roses of Virginia will die if transplanted.

King Edward the Sixth's perfume is made thusly: Take 12 spoonfuls of bright red Rose-water, the weight of sixpence in fine powder sugar, and boil it on hot embers and coals softly, and the room will smell as though it were full of Roses. But you must burn a sweet cypress wood before, to take away the gross air.

A love potion, made of red and white Rose leaves and Forget-me-nots, boiled in 385 drops of water for the sixteenth part of an hour, will, if properly made, insure the love of one of the opposite sex, if three drops of the mixture are put into something the person is to drink.

Moss

MATERNAL LOVE

HE Moss that covered the cross of King Oswald, of Northumbria, worked many miracles after that monarch's death. A citizen crossing the ice toward that venerated object fell and broke his arm; whereupon a friend tore some of the vegetation from the cross, clapped it on the injured member, and the bones knit instantly.

The Golden Moss of the Druids was a protection against unearthly creatures and black magic. This Moss was collected by the Druid nuns on the island of Sain, so that their warriors might use it to cover the tips of their arrows. The maiden who gathered the Moss was stripped of clothing, that she might better personify the Moon; she avoided iron, for if Moss touched that metal, calamity was near.

A poor child who had climbed the Fichtelgebirge in search of berries for her sick mother was met by a tiny Moss Creature who asked for some of the berries. The child cheerfully allowed the little woman to take her fill, and when the girl returned home she found that the remaining berries had turned to gold.

Headache may be removed by means of snuff made from the Moss which grows on a human skull in a Churchyard.

LILY

Purity of heart

Lily

NOTWITHSTANDING the great variety of the Lily's colors, we most readily associate this flower with *white:* for the poets have always linked this flower with purity and goodness. "What white," asks Browne, "can match the lily's virgin snows?" And so it has appeared to all the poets.

> *Have you seen but a bright lily grow*
> *Before rude hands have touched it?*
>
> BEN JONSON

The Greeks and Romans also regarded the Lily as a symbol of innocence, and they crowned new brides with Lilies and Wheat.

The Lily has remarkable powers in the land of Spain. Eating its petals will restore to human form any Spaniard who has been transformed to beastly shape; and the king of that land in 1048, on his death bed, beheld the Virgin walk forth from the Lily, at which sight he was restored to health.

To dream of Lilies in their season foretells marriage, happiness, and prosperity; but to dream of this flower in Winter indicates frustration of hopes, and the death of a beloved one.

Mr. Gerard's *Herball* offers two useful recipes using Lilies, to wit: "The root of the white Lily sod in honied water and dronken, driveth forth by the seige all corruptions of blood, as Pliny saith. The seed of Lillies is good to be dronken against the bite of serpents."

Sage
DOMESTIC VIRTUE

THE SAGE is highly esteemed for its healing properties; and its botanical name, *Salvia*, is derived from *salvo*, to heal. So wholesome was this herb considered that it was a common saying among men of an earlier age, *"Cur morietur homo cui Salvia crescit in horto?"* The sentiment thus expressed is found also in the English adage,

> *He who would live for aye*
> *Must eat Sage in May.*

Parkinson notes that "Sage is much used in the month of May, fasting, with butter and Parsley, and is held of most to conduce much to the health of man."

The peasants of Sussex eat Sage for nine consecutive mornings to rid themselves of ague-fits.

In every Sage leaf is concealed a toad, infinitely small. Such is the belief, at any rate, of Piedmontese girls, and the noted Turner states that "Rue is good to be planted amongst Sage, to prevent the poison which may be in it from toads frequenting amongst it, to relieve themselves of their poison, as is supposed; but Rue being amongst it, they will not come near it."

> *Plant your Sage and Rue together*
> *That Sage will grow in any weather.*

CAMELLIA
Perfected loveliness

Camellia

THE PURE whiteness of the Camellia and its absence of any odor, have long made it a symbol of purity, which is to say, *perfected loveliness*; such at any rate was its traditional representation, though M. Dumas *fils*, with the irony of the French, has used this flower to distinguish a woman of a very different sort indeed.

The leaves and blossoms of the Camellia resemble those of the Tea plant very closely, and the leaves of the two plants are sometimes mixed; not to deceive the purchaser of Tea, but to render its odor more delicate.

The introduction of the Camellia to Europe is the subject of a familiar story, and explains the origin of the name of this flower. It was brought to Queen Maria Theresa by the Moravian Jesuit, Kamel (or, Camelli), on his return from Asia. The Queen took the blooms to the King, who was then pacing the floor of his chamber in a fit of melancholy. Despite the flower's lack of fragrance, or perhaps because of this fact, Ferdinand pronounced the new flower a welcome member of his household; and the Camellia was assiduously cultivated in the hothouses of the palace. To honor the faithful monk, the flower was given his name.

Myrtle

THE MYRTLE being a flower of great importance to classical men and men of the classics, it is well that we note here what is known of its origin. The tree is derived from Myrene, a Grecian female and priestess, beloved of Venus who, to demonstrate her regard, made of her the Myrtle, which should be green throughout the year.

The Myrtle is thought by some to be the Whortleberry, a species much admired by the Finns and other Scandinavians. From the union of that mysterious berry with the goddess Ilma Tar they derive the origin of the Earth. Yet to believe this tale would perhaps be overly credulous.

To the Greeks, the Myrtle was the emblem of immortality; to the worldly Romans, it represented love. Thus, of all flowers, the Myrtle was barred from early religious festivals, for it was thought to encourage sensuality. In later times this property of the Myrtle has come to be respected, and it is said that a tea of Myrtle leaves makes a love philter capable of instigating and preserving love.

In Somersetshire the Myrtle is regarded as an uncommonly lucky plant, and one well worth preserving. It is there believed that one cannot induce a slip of Myrtle to grow unless one assumes a proud and haughty air while planting it, perhaps because of the proud heritage of which the Myrtle is conscious.

28

VIOLET
Faithfulness

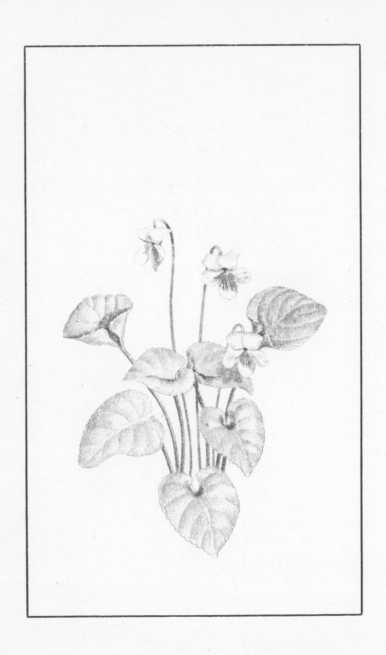

Violet

T HE VIOLET, as a symbol of Faithfulness, has been celebrated by no less a poet than Shakespeare himself:

Violet is for Faithfulness,
Which in me shall abide;
Hoping, likewise, that from your heart
You will not let it slide.

Some lovely maids of antiquity once became the objects of Venus' queenly wrath, when a dispute arose whether she or they were the more beautiful. Cupid judged in favor of the maidens; and in a fury, Venus beat them until they were blue. Thus the girls became the first Violets; this, anyway, is the story as Herrick tells it.

The most glorious of the Greeks regarded the Violet with extreme favor, and preferred for themselves above all other names, that of "Athenian crowned with Violets."

A garland of Violets, worn about the head, prevents dizziness.

Where roses and violets bloom in Autumn, an epidemic will follow within the year.

Bullein's advice concerning Violets is as follows: "Take of the water of Violet flowers, of fine Sugar sodden and clarified, mingle them, and seethe therein with a soft fire. This is a pleasant remedy in all burning Agues."

31

Edelweiss

PERSEVERANCE

HE MODEST Edelweiss, or "noble white," is of its nature so self-effacing that it might well be overlooked were it not that it is a favorite of poor Swiss urchins who pick clumps to sell, and of tourists to the Alps who buy them.

The prevalence of this flower in the Alpine regions is explained by an old tale. An angel, longing to visit once more her home on earth, was allowed to reassume her human form; as a beautiful maiden she descended, striking first upon the Alps, most proximate to the heavenly regions. There she was discovered by some mountain climbers, who were so struck by her consummate beauty that they prayed to God to remove the temptation of the angel's loveliness, since they could not possess her supernatural spirit. The angel was transformed into the Edelweiss, and in that form she remains to this day.

Because the Edelweiss grows only at the snow line upon the Alps, it is considered an act of daring to return with it from the heights; therefore it is much prized by Swiss maidens, who regard it as proof of the affections of any young man who will bring it to them.

So popular, in fact, is the custom of plucking the Edelweiss that strict regulations have been passed forbidding the practice, so that the precious flower will not be made extinct by its very admirers. Outside the usual tourist routes, however, the Edelweiss grows in such abundance that it is used as food for cattle.

LOTUS
Eloquence

VERITABLE wealth of symbolic meanings is attached to the Lotus; it would not be wrong to say that it is the most widely interpreted flower in the Orient. The flower is sacred, for it was on the Lotus that Brahma alighted when he sprang from the navel of Vishnu. From that beginning he ordered the existence of all worlds. Thus the Lotus represents the world; though it has the further associations of the Sun, the Moon, female beauty, and silence.

Egyptians eat a bread made from Lotus kernels, as do the Chinese, and their poets sing of the Lotus-eaters, who grow so attached to their divine food that they remain where it grows, and care for nothing else in all the world.

One King Pându, who mocked the holy relics of the Buddhists, attempted to burn a tooth of Buddha; but there sprang from the flames a Lotus flower, and the tooth was found lying on its petals.

The people of Eastern India give the Lotus eighteen names, which describe the eighteen different beauties of the god Brahma; and the god is said to sleep in the petals of the Lotus six months of the year.

The Lotus was first described in the West by Herodotus, who mentions the "water lily that grows in the inundated lands of Egypt." The Lotus typifies Lower Egypt, as the papyrus represents Upper Egypt.

Laurel

GLORY

THE LAUREL, long the emblem of emperors and victorious athletes, was created in this fashion; Daphne, daughter of the river Peneus, was offended by the persecutions of Apollo; at her request, the gods changed her into a Laurel tree. Apollo fashioned a wreath of the leaves, and declared that henceforth the tree should be sacred to him.

Dispatches from victorious Roman generals to the Senate were wrapped in Laurel leaves.

Among the Ancients, when a poet read his verses at a university, he was crowned with Laurel; from this custom derived the word, baccalaureate, which means, Laurel berry.

Our ancestors held great faith in the power of the Laurel to avert evil. Indeed, Emperor Tiberius set such store by the leaves that whenever a storm arose he seized a Laurel crown and crawled under the bed for safety.

Burning of Laurel leaves is a frequent recourse of maidens who wish to win back the attentions of errant lovers.

On the death of Nero, all Laurel trees withered to the root.

CHRYSANTHEMUM
Cheerfulness in adversity

Chrysanthemum

Originally in the Chinese domain, the Chrysanthemum has since been brought to Japan, where it receives adulation not often accorded any flower. To the Japanese the Chrysanthemum, or *kiku*, as they call it, symbolizes the sun; and the orderly unfolding of its petals represents perfection. An annual festival in Japan is devoted to the *kiku*, at which florists vie with each other to produce the most striking displays and the most original strains of this flower.

Another tradition of the Japanese with regard to the Chrysanthemum is the belief that one of its petals, placed in the bottom of a wine glass, encourages longevity.

Relatives of the Chrysanthemum found naturally in England have assumed the character of weeds; these being the Corn Marigold, the Ox-eye Daisy, and the Feverfew. The last of these was once much admired for its physic properties; though perhaps through the contempt bred by familiarity it has had to bear an uncommon number of rude names, such as Arse-smart, Stink Daisies, and Nosebleed.

More recently the true Chrysanthemum has been widely recognized in England and America as a prize for garden fanciers. Careful and judicious breeding has produced literally hundreds of new species.

Passion Flower

FAITH

THE PASSION FLOWER is native to America, and so named because it is emblematic of the Passion of Christ. Its ten petals represent the ten Apostles aside from Judas and Peter; the purple threads surrounding the style suggest the crown of thorns; and the style itself represents the column to which the malefactors were bound. Furthermore, the three divisions at the top of the style represent the three nails. One of the stamens being taken for a hammer, the remaining four form the Cross. The time between the opening and closing of this flower being three days completes the representation.

It is an old Spanish belief that after the Crucifixion, the Passion Flower climbed upon the Cross and covered the marks in the wood left by the nails. When Spanish missionaries found this flower growing in the wilds of America, it seemed to them a proof that the natives should be converted.

When this flower was introduced in Europe, in 1600, and the Jesuits announced that it was the floral representation of the Passion, an indignant botanist objected, saying "I dare say God never willed His priests to instruct His people with lies; for they come from the Devill, the author of them." In our calmer day the beauties of this flower delight Protestants as much as other men.

DAFFODIL
Regard

Daffodil

THE DAFFODIL, while a close relation of the ill-fated Narcissus, is much admired in its own right, and widely celebrated by our poets. Thus, in his famous eulogy, Milton commands,

> Bid Amaranthus all his beauty shed
> And daffodillies fill their cups with tears
> To strew the laureat hearse where Lycid lies.

Spenser repeatedly notices this flower:

> Strew me the ground with daffodowndillies
> With cowslips, and king-cups, and loved lillies.

By many the Daffodil is regarded as a harbinger of the Springtime, as in the famous verse of Shakespeare,

> When Daffodils begin to peer,
> With heigh! the doxy o'er the dale
> Why, then comes in the sweet o' the year.

A distillation of the Daffodil has been beneficially used as an embrocation in dropsy and palsy.

We learn from Pliny, however, that "The Ointment Narcissum, where the flower of the Daffodil was the Basis, is now forgotten, and no more made of it."

Woodbine

FRATERNAL LOVE

OODBINE, or Virginia Creeper, is beloved of witches, primarily; and yet the greatest poets of our tongue have sung its praises. In olden times, consumptive invalids or children suffering from hectic fever were passed thrice through a circular wreath of Woodbine, cut during the increase of the March moon and let down over the body from head to foot. We read of a sorceress who healed sundry women by taking a garland of green Woodbine and causing the patient to pass thrice through it: afterwards the garland was cut in nine pieces, and cast in the fire. Woodbine appears to have been a favorite with Scottish witches, who, in effecting magical cures, passed their patients (generally) nine times through a girth or garland of green Woodbine.

According to the astrologers, Woodbine is in alliance with Mercury.

PANSY
I think of thee

Pansy

THE SIGNIFICANCE or language of the Pansy is indeed well remarked; for our name for this modest flower derives in fact from the French *pensée*, denoting "thought" to those of a Gallic turn of mind. And it would seem that the language of the Pansy is known in Denmark, as well; certainly we all remember poor Ophelia's parting wish,

> *pray you, love, remember*
> *There's pansies—that's for thoughts.*

The Pansy once had as fine a perfume as a flower might wish: but this sweet fragrance made the Pansy so much in demand that people plucked it almost to extinction. It is reported that during these years some peasants of Saxony even made food of the Pansy. In despair, the Pansy appealed to the Trinity that it might lose its odor, and be no longer sought. The prayer was granted, and ever since the Pansy has been regarded as the flower of the Trinity.

The stamens and pistil of this flower have something grotesque in their appearance, suggesting to a fanciful mind an animal with arms and head projecting. The Wild Pansy is commonly called Heartsease.

"How shall a blind man tell the color of a pansy?" asks Locke, always acute.

Cactus

WARMTH

THE CACTUS, while at first of forbidding aspect, has in fact many qualities that commend it to man's affection; and this is very likely why it is considered a sign of warmth. The Aztecs who founded Mexico were told by their wise men to establish their new city where they found an eagle, a snake, and a Cactus: and in this manner they established Mexico City at its present site. The ability of the Cactus to store water in desert regions is well known. Another useful property of this plant is the role it plays in the incantations of Voodoo men, who use its thorns to immolate the images of their enemies, causing great injury to the person represented.

While the Cactus is basically a thorny and injurious plant by appearance, it has flowers of rare beauty, seldom seen by those of us who dwell in the temperate regions. Of these the flower of *Cactus speciosissimus* is of unrivaled splendor: this flower is the subject of Mrs. Sigourney's justly popular poem.

The first Cactus plant known in Europe, exhibited in Spain by returning explorers in 1590, caused the Queen to turn pale with fright; but when this plant was shown to contain water saved from the American desert, it was accounted a great miracle.

The thorn of a Cactus growing alone, when carried with the person on a string, preserves health and well-being in the face of danger.

FORGET-ME-NOT
True love

Forget-Me-Not

THE MEANING of the Forget-me-not is easily seen from its name; and there is a story explaining how the name came to be. A young man and his maid walked one day along the Danube, when the girl spied some lovely flowers on the opposite bank and made known her desire for them. The youth swam the stream, picked a bunch of the precious blossoms, and struck out again across the raging river. A huge wave bore down upon him and carried him off toward the Black Sea. It was all he could do to fling the bouquet at the feet of his beloved, crying, "Forget me not!" as he disappeared from view. The maiden made a chain of the flowers which she wore always; and she never forgot him, if legend can be believed.

If one takes a sojourn in Egypt near the 27th day of their month Thoth (which is near to our month of August), and he anoints his eyes with the flower Forget-me-not, he will be made to see visions. At least so it was in ancient times.

It is thought among the Germans, who lack perhaps the element of romance in their floral legends, that the name "Forget-me-not" derives from the nauseous taste which that flower leaves in the mouth. Yet these same Germans are apt to plant the Forget-me-not on their graves, so as to be remembered; which seems to indicate some caprice or else irony of spirit.

IRIS
Message

Iris

HE IRIS is often known as the *fleur-de-lys*, a name of royal derivation. Louis the Seventh, having distinguished himself in the Second Crusade, chose a particular blazon to appear on his coat-of-arms; this being, in fact, the Iris. The common people contracted the name of Louis to Luce, and then finally to Lys: and in time the Iris assumed the name of its royal admirer.

Clotilda, wife of warlike Clovis, long prayed for the conversion of her husband during the early years of the sixth century. Once Clovis led his army against the Huns, and, being in imminent danger of defeat, recommended himself to the God of his sainted wife. A victory was the outcome, and Clovis was baptized. On this occasion he substituted the Iris for the three toads which had always appeared on his shield.

A pious old peasant, having become, from conviction, a monk, was too old for saintly "book learning," and never could manage to remember more than two words of a single prayer, these being *Ave Maria*. On his death, the fleur-de-lys sprang up on his grave, bearing those words inscribed upon it. The monks, who had scorned their fellow, regarded the event as a miracle.

Acanthus
ARTIFICE

THE ACANTHUS was perpetuated for us by the ancients in the form of the Corinthian column, which takes its shape from this flower. How it happened is on this wise: A sweet young maid of Corinth died and was buried in a spot where grew the Acanthus. Her old nurse placed on her grave the child's fondest possessions, her toys and ornaments, around which the Acanthus flowers grew up. The great sculptor Callimachus happened by, and, charmed by the form the leaves took, carved the column in their image.

Virgil tells us that the Acanthus flower was the basis of the design decorating Helen's mantle, which may have been, in view of the loveliness of this flower, the attraction Paris found there—or so we may imagine.

An old name for the Acanthus is "Bear's Breech," which epithet this flower shares with the Cow Parsnip.

It has been suggested that the Acanthus formed Christ's crown of thorns, although this sad distinction is more often conferred on the Bramble or Rose-Briar.

CROCUS
Abuse not

Crocus

E PRIZE the Crocus as the first flower to spring from the earth after the cold of Winter; much as did the first Crocus, if it were not to draw too close a connection, spring from the warmth of the body of Zeus on a bank on Mount Ida, after he had lain there with Juno. For such was the origin of this flower, if we can believe the teachings of the Greeks.

The juice of the Crocus was in much favor among the women of Rome for its use as a hair-dye, though this practice later received the censure of the Church fathers. The Irish were wont to use the Crocus as a dye for linens, until forbidden to do so by Henry VIII.

The lovely Saffron Crocus was the exclusive joy of the rajah of Kashmir for many years. In the time of Edward III, however, a forehanded English traveler secreted one of the bulbs of the plant in a hollow staff, and so brought the flower to the West.

The Crocus has been considered useful in the plague and similar pestilences; and there are those who vouch for its efficacy as a stimulant of the passions.

Thornapple

DECEITFUL CHARMS

HE THORNAPPLE is a mystic plant, resembling the Mandrake in its powers; Gerard believes it to be the *Hippomanes* of Theocritus, which caused horses to go mad.

The juice of Thornapples, boiled with hog's grease, makes a benevolent salve which heals burns and scaldings "as well of fire, water, boiling lead, gunpowder, as that which comes by lightning."

In India thieves and robbers make clever use of this plant. They cunningly induce their victims to eat thereof, whereupon those who obey become giddy and openhearted, allowing anyone to pillage them. For somewhat similar purposes, Indian dancing girls are known to mix the juice of this herb with wine.

It is believed elsewhere in the Orient that goats who eat this plant behave very strangely, attempting to walk on two feet as a human being.

GERANIUM
I shall never see him

Geranium

E HAVE in our lanes and gardens a great profusion of Geraniums, and a great diversity of species. Yet the people who have done the Geranium the most honor are the men of the Orient. There it is a sacred plant, and its origin is told thusly: One day when Mahomet was traveling, he washed his shirt and hung it upon a hedge to dry while he said his prayers. Upon removing his shirt, he found the common hedge transformed into the beautiful Geranium; so great was the divinity of that prophet.

A wild variety of the Geranium is known in England, where it is called "herb Robert"; which name seems to derive either from Robin Hood, the noted highwayman, or from Saint Robert, the founder of the Cistercian Order. It was this holy man, in any case, who used the Geranium to cure Ruprecht's Plague.

Gerard found the odor of the Geranium objectionable and described it as "a most lothsome stinking smell"; but this flower also had its medicinal uses, chiefly for the staying of the blood, though it is also given to cattle suffering from red water.

The properties of Dove's Foot, a variety of the Geranium, are even more striking. Gerard found it of marvellous worth against ruptures, when powdered and drunk in red wine or old claret. If the rupture was in an old person, he added, the flower should be fortified with the powder of nine red slugs, dried in an oven.

Mistletoe

DIFFICULTIES SURMOUNTED

THE MISTLETOE was the sacred plant of the Druids, and much used in all their rites. From this circumstance, the Priests have forbidden its admission into Christian churches; but on Christmas Eve it is hung up in the kitchen, subjecting every female who passes under it to a salute from any young man who may be present.

In Germany, if you will carry a sprig of Mistletoe into an old house, the ghosts who live there will appear to you, and by means of it you may force them to answer questions. A sprig of Mistletoe above the bed will ward away nightmares from the French; in Sweden, a finger-ring made of its wood is an antidote to sickness.

The delicate Mistletoe was formerly a sturdy tree, until its wood was used for Christ's cross.

Fresh Mistletoe-berries (not exceeding nine in number) steeped in a liquid composed of equal proportions of wine, beer, vinegar, and honey, taken as pills on an empty stomach before going to bed, will cause dreams of your future destiny (providing you retire to rest before twelve) either on Christmas Eve or on the first and third of a new moon.

ASTER

Afterthought; variety

THE NAME of the Aster, signifying *star* in Latin, directs our thoughts and aspirations ever upward. The old name for this flower, not quite so delicate, perhaps, is "Star-wort."

Virgil tells us that the altars of the gods were often adorned with these flowers. In his fourth Georgic, the poet prescribes the root of the Aster as a physic for sickly bees.

The odor of the leaves of the Aster, when burnt, will drive away serpents.

It is interesting to note that the oracle for determining a lover's fidelity, associated for us with the Daisy in the saying "He loves me—loves me not," appears in Germany as an oracle of the Aster. The German maidens pluck the petals of this flower, as do their English sisters, saying,

> *Er liebt mich von Herzen*
> *Mit Schmerzen*
> *Ja—oder Nein . . .*

We may hope that the Aster gives a favorable response as often as does the Daisy.

The Sea Aster, a relative, is said by Gerard to be proof against dropsy and poisons.

POPPY

Fantastic extravagance

Poppy

THE PRIME significance of the Poppy, and that which has given it fame among men, both ancient and modern, is its soporific power. The origin of this faculty of the Poppy is described in Hesiod, who tells us that Poppies grew at the entrance to Somnus' murky cave; and that Somnus himself lay on a couch, attended by Dreams and by Morpheus, who held a vase in one hand, and a bunch of Poppies in the other.

Livy tells us that when Sextus heard from a messenger that Tarquin had cut off the heads of the tallest Poppies in his garden, he took this as sufficient hint to poison the chief men of the Gabii.

The frightening mystery of the Poppy is oft expressed by our poets, perhaps by none so well as by Drayton:

> Here henbane, poppy, hemlock here,
> Procuring deadly sleeping:
> Which I do minister by fear;
> Not fit for each man's keeping.

Lord Bacon showed himself to have a higher regard for peace and quiet than for the health of his children when he recommended that Poppy-seeds be added to their food.

Henbane

IMPERFECTION

THE COMMON Henbane is the black variety, which bears pale, woolly, clammy leaves, with venomous-looking cream-colored flowers, and has a foetid smell. Pliny rightly marks this plant as one of evil omens, employed in funeral repasts, black masses, and festivals of witches.

The ancients felt great fear of this plant, believing that if anyone ate it, sterility would be the result. Henbane was called *Insana*, as anyone eating it became stupid and drowsy; and also *Alterculum*, because those who had eaten it became quarrelsome.

Henbane is sometimes prescribed for the liver complaints of horses. Sheep and goats eat this plant sparingly, but swine are said really to like it.

Henbane's place in Dentistry is described by Gerard: "The root boiled with vinegre, and the same holden hot in the mouth, easeth the pain of teeth. The seed is used by mountebank tooth-drawers, which run about the country, to cause worms to come forth of the teeth, by burning it in a chafing-dish of coles, the party holding his mouth over the fume thereof; but some crafty companions, to gain money, convey small lute-strings into the water, persuading the patient that those small creepers came out of his mouth or other parts which he intended to cure."

SUNFLOWER
False appearance

Sunflower

EING SUCH an obvious symbol of the Lord of the Day, the Sunflower was much esteemed by the sun-worshipers of Peru. Their priestesses in the sun-temples wore copies of these flowers in gold, to the great joy of the Spaniards, who immediately possessed themselves of these shocking evidences of heathenism—and put the reprobate priestesses to the sword.

If a girl puts three Sunflower-seeds down her back, she will marry the first boy she meets.

The Sunflower is a symbol of devout feeling, for it turns its visage ever toward the sun, bowing humbly at sunset. It is this fact to which Moore refers in his pious verse:

The Sunflower turns to her god, when he sets,
The same look which she turned when he rose.

The natives of the Island of Corfu are reported to wear Sunflowers as hats.

Amaranth

FOPPERY

OUR REPRESENTATION of the Amaranth comes more properly from the Crested Amaranth, or "Coxcomb," which flower by its crest has so haughty an appearance as to seem to approach human conceit. Thus, "The painted coxcomb his beauties vaunting," says the poet; although this flower is truly so fair that it deserves a more amiable sobriquet.

The Amaranth was a sacred flower among the Greeks and Romans, associated with immortality. Homer tells us that the Thessalians wore crowns of Amaranth at Achilles' funeral.

While many flowers are prized for their ability to excite romantic feeling, the Amaranth, either ground to powder or in a potion, has from the time of Pliny been used to *curb the affections*.

That species of Amaranth most commonly found in our gardens, known to us as "Love lies a-bleeding," is in France given the singular name of "The nun's scourge."

A wreath of Amaranth made in Switzerland on Ascension Day makes the wearer invisible.

NARCISSUS
Self-love

VERY READER is familiar with the heritage of the Narcissus. This fateful flower is named for Narcissus, a youth of ancient times, who became so enamored of his own reflection, perceived in a fountain, that he pined and took his life. His blood, according to Ovid, was changed into a flower. This tragic event has been much celebrated by the poets, as in the following lines:

> *As when the chilling east invades the spring,*
> *The delicate narcissus pines away*
> *In hectic langour, and a slow disease*
> *Taints all the family of flowers* . . .

Ancient writers referred to the Narcissus as a flower of deceit; for it is reputed to have narcotic properties. Thus Homer assures us that the flower delights heaven and earth by its odor and beauty, yet that it produces at the same time stupor, madness, and even death.

A crown of these flowers was often worn by the Greeks in honor of the infernal gods, and placed upon the heads of the dead.

As the French Poet declares: "Narcisse oriental, fleur inféconde et pas morale."

Dandelion
COQUETRY

THE NAME Dandelion is a corruption of the French *Dent de lion;* for it may be that the Gauls of old fancied some resemblance between the jagged leaf and the regal jaw of the beast. However this may be, our associations with this modest flower are of a gentler nature. The custom of blowing its seeds, to carry thoughts toward a loved one, is well established. Much that is good can be made of this plant, both food and medicine; and it is well known that the inhabitants of Minorca once subsisted for weeks on this plant when their harvest was entirely destroyed by insects.

A most superior coffee can be made of Dandelion roots, which are a staple food in many parts of the world. The roots should be dug up in Autumn, washed, cut in pieces, and dried in the sun. They can be stored until needed; then they are roasted and used.

If the down flies off a Dandelion when there is no wind, it is a sure sign of rain.

To dream of Dandelions portends ill fortune.

The Dandelion was associated by Helvetius with the Teeth and the Spleen.

Mr. John Gay finds a place for the Dandelion in an elegy:

Let dandelions spread;
For Blouzelinda, blithesome maid, is dead!

APPLE

Temptation

Apple

THE FRUIT which is born of the beautiful Apple blossom plays a part in our oldest and most famous legends. It has long been considered the sweet prize with which the Serpent tempted our first ancestors; for though we are not told that the Apple was the fruit "good for food and pleasant to the eyes," we nevertheless think it so. For the Apple, Atalanta lost her famous race; and it is the Apple for which Tantalus must ever reach in vain. Thus our modest Apple is truly the symbol of *Temptation*; and to send a bouquet of Apple Blossoms is to say, "I am tempted."

The fruit of the Apple is useful in many charms and divinations dear to maidens, an example of which is that if an Apple is cut in half on Christmas Eve, the left half being placed in the bosom and the right half by the door, the Desired Person will be found near the right half at midnight.

Apple twigs planted upside-down will bear Apples without cores.

Man's love for the Apple tree is best demonstrated in the Apple Wassail festivals on Christmas Eve. Farmers in the remoter districts of England still practice this ceremony, in which the people come from Church into the orchards to sprinkle cider on a representative tree, then chant a toast.

Marigold

GRIEF

OR a definition of the Marigold, we can look to no higher an authority than Dr. Johnson, who tells us that "The marygold is a yellow flower, devoted to the Virgin Mary."

"In drawing most flowers, you must first produce a circle, as for the rose, and the marigold."—Peacham. A more practical consideration is offered by Edgeworth, that "In England, the petals of the garden marigold are much used in soups." "Fair is the marigold, for pottage meet," says Gay.

The Marigold is considered by many authors the emblem of jealousy and fawning; and we are told that the first of these flowers sprang from a maiden who was so consumed with envy at the success of her rival that she lost her wits and perished.

Linnaeus tells us that the Marigold is normally opened from 9 A.M. until 3 P.M., and that an early closing of its petals foretells rain. The head of this flower turns perpetually toward the Sun, which circumstance inspired Marguerite of Orleans to choose for her armorial device a Marigold turning toward the Sun, with the motto "Je ne veux suivre que lui seul."

The Marigold is sometimes called Death Flower in America, after the tradition that it sprang from the blood of those unfortunate Mexicans who were crazed by the love of gold.

LUPINE
Voraciousness

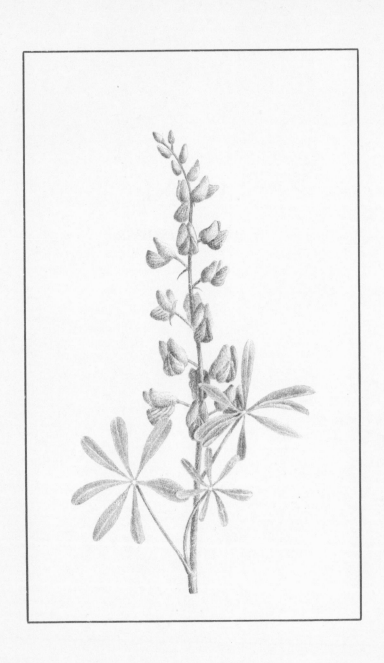

Lupine

THE ROMANS cultivated the Lupine for its food value, and Pliny declares that nothing is more wholesome than white Lupines eaten dry. This diet was said to impart fresh color and a cheerful countenance.

The eating of this flower was also thought to stimulate one's mental powers. It is said that Protogenes, the noted painter of Rhodes, subsisted for seven years on a diet of Lupines and water while painting the hunting piece of Ialysus, with the idea that this food would give him greater flights of fancy.

The seeds of the Lupine were used by the ancients in their dramatic productions, as stage money; hence the proverb, *Nummus Lupinus*, which is to say a worthless coin.

The Lupine is commonly called the Sundial, as its leaves follow the Sun in his course. So it is that the Lupine directs a little maid out of a wood in the poem by Miss Edgarton:

> *She cast her dim eyes downwards*
> *And O, with what delight*
> *Discerned a little Lupine*
> *Soft smiling through the night!*

Nettle

CRUELTY

THE HATEFUL venom of the Nettle has on at least one occasion been thought to turn to some good account, when Roman soldiers journeying to Britain brought seeds of this plant with them. The leaves being cultivated, they were rubbed on the limbs in extreme cold, so as to warm the blood in the unaccustomed chills of the North.

To pluck a Nettle by the root three successive mornings before sunrise brings relief from the Ague.

To cure the sting of the Nettle in Scotland, one must rub the affected part with leaves of Dock, saying, "Nettle in, Dock out; Dock rub Nettle out."

Nettles gathered before sunrise will drive evil spirits from cattle.

Nettle-seed is used in Germany to excite the passions and to facilitate birth.

"He that handles a Nettle tenderly is soonest stung."

MORNING GLORY
Affectation

Morning Glory

THE LEAVES of the Morning Glory, mashed and boiled, make a poultice sometimes applied to the face for treatment of mumps. Yet Gerard counsels against this practice, saying of the Morning Glory that "It is not fit for medicine, an unprofitable weed and hurtful to each thing that groweth next it, and only administered by runnagat physickmongers, quacksalvers, old women leeches, abusers of physick and deceivers of people."

The Morning Glory shares with several flowers the property of opening and closing its flowers to mark the passing of the day; thus it is known as a "shepherd's clock."

The English seem less charitable to the Morning Glory than are we, calling it by the unfriendly name of Bindweed. Indeed, many gardeners will have spent days of labor trying to rid their flower beds of this handsome but greedy interloper. But one must be careful never to burn the vines of the Morning Glory or Bindweed: for if they crack and sputter, it is a sign that someone present will die.

Clematis
ARTFULNESS

CLEMATIS, called "traveler's joy," has many useful properties. It is used by small boys as a substitute for tobacco, filling homemade pipes and cigars. Professional mendicants in certain European countries use this plant as an aid to their deceitful beggary. Clematis secretes an irritating juice, which, rubbed into a small cut in the skin, causes a large superficial sore. These feigned injuries will often draw a contribution of alms from unsuspecting benefactors.

The French peasant wife is likely to make a clothes-line out of the Clematis vine.

It is said that the Nightingale sings at night so as to keep himself awake; for otherwise he would be caught fast by the climbing vines of the Clematis. Thus his song, as rendered by the French becomes

Je ne dormirai plus, plus, plus . . .
M'entortillerait la vigne!

The Clematis is sometimes known as "Virgin's Bower," out of respect for Queen Elizabeth, and with reference to its climbing properties.

Miller tells us that if a leaf of *Clematis flammula* be picked on a hot Summer's day, crushed, and presently put in the nose, it will cause a burning sensation much like a flame.

PRIMROSE

Inconstancy

Primrose

WELL IS the Primrose esteemed a mark of *Inconstancy;* for while it is a charming flower, bringing to Mankind the first tidings of Springtime, it can turn against him with many a poison.

Thus has the poet, Keats, mentioned with favor a near relative of this flower:

A tuft of Evening Primroses
O'er which the wind may hover till it dozes;
O'er which it well might take a pleasant sleep;
But that 't is ever startled by the leap
Of buds into ripe flowers.

And yet we are told that a pretty variety, *Primula obconica,* does utter a poisonous exhalation, likely to cause headache and rash on hands and face. So do the manners of this bloom change with her circumstances, and in this trait she is well likened to Woman herself, if we are to believe the testimony of many of our authors.

It is exceedingly unlucky in Springtime to take less than a handful of Primroses or Violets into a farmer's house; for disregard of this rule invites destruction of the good wife's brood of ducklings and chickens.

The goddess Bertha is supposed to entice children to enter her enchanted halls by offering them beautiful Primroses.

Dahlia
INSTABILITY

HE DAHLIA is noted as the favorite flower of Josephine, Empress of the French; so great was the pleasure she took in this flower that it was cultivated at Malmaison almost to the exclusion of any other blooms. The pride that the great take in our modest flowers is often a jealous passion; and like many before her, Josephine forbade that anyone take root or seed of her Dahlias. One day a Polish prince succeeded in gaining for himself a hundred of these plants, through judicious coin passed across the gardener's palm; at which event Josephine declared herself so greatly revolted by the sight of her once-precious Dahlias that she never wished to see one again. We have not all the burden of such petulance.

In Germany and Russia the Dahlia is called "Georgina," after a St. Petersburg professor.

This flower, the favorite of many crowned heads of Europe, is native to Mexico, where it has long decorated the most humble peasant's garden.

The passion of the French Empress for the Dahlia has been remarked above. Her feeling for this flower was popularly known, and was in fact the subject of a quatrain by one of Napoleon's political enemies:

> *Vos Dahlias, auguste Madame,*
> *Me serrent d'un effroi imprécis:*
> *Faut-il tenir au centre de l'âme*
> *Une fleure si amère que celle ci?*

CORNFLOWER
Quarrel

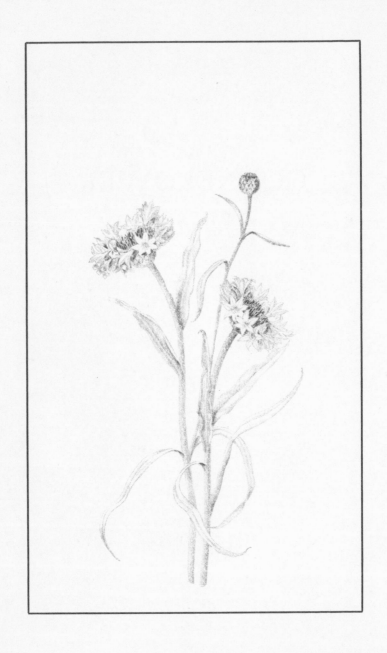

Cornflower

THE CORNFLOWER, so called because, like the poppy, it grows among the corn stalks, is known among the English, and perhaps more properly, as the "Centaury." This name is in honor of Chiron, the famous centaur, who recovered from the poison of an arrow dipped in the blood of the hundred-headed hydra by covering the wound with these small blue flowers.

The Cornflower, or *Centaurea*, has more recently been the emblem of the German imperial family, established as such by the Emperor Wilhelm. As a child, the Emperor had lain hidden in a field with his mother, Queen Louise of Prussia, before Napoleon's advance; and when Wilhelm turned the tables on the third Napoleon, he remembered the Cornflowers he had lain among, and made this flower his signet.

The odors of burned Cornflowers will drive away spirits.

According to the old herbalists, an infusion of Cornflowers has the power to remove freckles.

The virtues of the Cornflower as a physic are widely regarded. Gerard, always an authority, tells us that when Cornflower blossoms are "gathered superstitiouslie, they are gathered between the two ladiedaies," but that, in any case, they are good against dropsy and weakness, with "a peculiar vertue against infirmities of the sinews." Lady Wilkinson suggests that medical use of the Cornflower has probably done "more good and less harm than any other popular 'simple.' "

Basil

HATRED

THE NAME Basil means *king*, for thus Royalty were designated by the Greeks in their language. It may be also called the "King over pain," for at times its medicinal properties have enjoyed the highest respect. Other ages have called this plant an evil poison, and it would seem that the latter opinion prevailed when the Basil was chosen to signify *Hatred*. In the Orient, Basil is a holy and religious herb; for the Hindus bury their dead with a sprig of Basil to admit them to heaven, and the Persians plant Basil over their graves to make the dead appealing to the gods.

It is commonly known that if a Rumanian girl desire the affections of a young man, she need only get him to accept some Basil from her hand, and he will be ever faithful to her.

So closely is the powerful Basil thought to lie with Hatred, that the ancients believed it could only be sown when accompanied by curses and imprecations. We have as further evidence the expression "to sow Basil," which means "to slander."

Lord Bacon tells us that if Basil is exposed to excessive sunlight, it changes into Wild Thyme; but this curious notion has never been proven.

Gerard testifies that the smell of Basil is good for the heart and for the head.

100

PEONY
Shame

Peony

O F ALL the flowers valued for their medicinal properties, the Peony is among the first and the most famous. The name of this flower is a celebration of Apollo Physician, who as Paeon healed the wounds received by the gods in the Trojan War. It has long been a custom to wear about the neck a chain of beads carved from Peony roots, as a protection against all manner of illness and injury, and in the case of children, to assist them in teething.

Pliny tells us that the Peony is of all flowers the favorite of the Woodpecker; and that if this fierce bird sees anyone picking the flower's blooms, he will peck out the eyes of the offender.

The crimson blush of the Peony is not considered a sign of modesty, but a mark of shame commemorating the vanquishing of a shepherdess by the Sun god. From this we derive the significance of this flower, which is Shame, or disrepute.

Worn on the person, the Peony is an effective remedy for insanity. And Lord Bacon affirms its excellence against the falling sickness, whose cause "is the grossness of the vapours, which rise and enter into the cells of the brain."

St. Johnswort

O N THE 29th day of August, when St. John was beheaded, the flower bearing that Saint's name shows its red spots. The St. Johnswort is known also as Devil Chaser, because if it is hung in windows on the 24th of June, the Saint's birthday, it will repel ghosts, devils, imps, and thunderbolts.

Yet if one should step on this herb in the fields of the Isle of Wight he must beware; for a phantom horse will rise from its root, taking the visitor on its back, and ride away all through the night wherever it pleases.

If, on the eve of St. John, a maid of Lower Saxony hang St. Johnswort upon her wall, and it remain fresh until the following morning, the girl can expect a proposal of marriage within the year; but if the flowers have wilted, she will do well to pursue other purposes until the next June.

B. Visontius recommends this herb as a cure for heart melancholy, when gathered on a Friday, in the hour of Jupiter; "so gathered, and borne or hung about the neck, it mightily helps this affection, and drives away all phantastical spirits."

THISTLE
Austerity

Thistle

HE THISTLE is a harsh plant; yet it carries itself with the beauty of nobility. It is often associated with grief, and the story of its origin bears out this connection. When Daphnis, shepherd and musician, passed from the Earth, the rustic Chloe made the Thistle as a token of her love for him, its beautiful flowers lying among the thorns of sadness.

The Thistle proved the saving of Charlemagne's army when it was struck by an epidemic. The gratitude of the French was so great that in the fourteenth century they founded the Order of the Thistle, dedicated to the Virgin. With its thorns removed, cooked as a vegetable, the Thistle acts as a specific against ague and jaundice; and, taken in wine, it "expels superfluous melancholy out of the body and makes a man as merry as a cricket."

The Thistle has been adopted as the national symbol of the Scots because during the Danish wars a party of Danes advanced barefooted upon the sleeping Scots, and would have killed them had not one of the marauders stepped on a Thistle and given a shout of pain. The Scots awoke and defeated the invaders; and they forthwith made the Thistle their emblem, with the motto *Nemo me impune lacessit.*

LILY OF THE VALLEY
Return to happiness

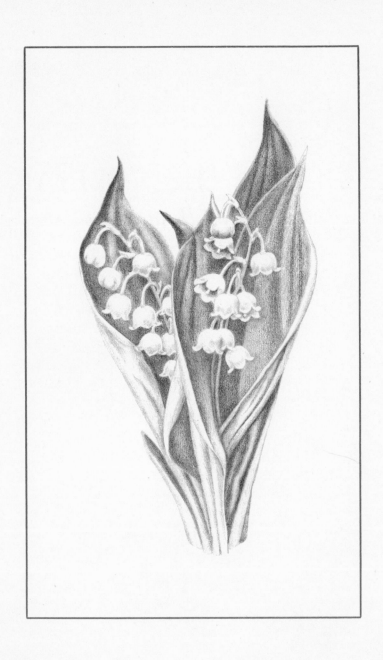

Lily of The Valley

HE SMALL and precious flowers of the Lily of the Valley trace their origin in fact to a fierce battle between a holy man and a hideous beast. One day in the woods St. Leonard met with the great dragon, Malitia; upon sight of each other the upholders of good and evil began a fearsome struggle. For fully three days they fought, neither seeming to give quarter; but when the dawn of the fourth day broke, the patron of all that is horrible began to slink away into the forest. He left a trail of blood, the hard-won spoils of the Saint, and where this blood lay it was sanctified by heaven and became Lilies of the Valley.

Water distilled from these flowers is effective medicine against all nervous diseases; indeed it was once so highly prized that it was kept only in silver and gold containers. Camerarius prescribes an oil of these flowers against gout: "Have filled a glass with flowers, and being well stopped, set it for a moneth's space in an ante's hill, and after being drayned cleare, set it by for use."

The flowers of this plant, dried and powdered, are used to excite sneezing.

Gerard informs us that the roots of Solomon's Seal, a relation, will take away "any bruse, blacke or blewe spotts, gotten by falls, or woman's wilfulnesse in stumbling on their hastie husbande's fists, or such like."

REFERENCER
To Symbolic Meaning by Flowers

(Those Blossoms or Plants
designated by *italics* are allotted
a page of description of their properties,
various nomenclatures, etc., at
the pages indicated in the
preceding text.)

Acanthus — Artifice; Fine Arts [56].

Amaranth — Affectation; Foppery [76].

Amaryllis — Pride; Timidity.

Anemone — Abandonment; Expectation; Refusal;
Sickness.

Apple — Temptation [83].

Aster — Afterthought; Daintiness; Elegance; Variety
[67].

Azalia — Fragile, Ephemeral Passion; Temperance.

Bachelor's Button — Celibacy.

Balsam — Impatience.

Basil — Hatred [100].

Belladonna — Silence.

Buttercup — Ingratitude; Mockery; Sarcasm.

Cactus — Bravery; Endurance; Warmth [48].

Camellia — Excellence; Perfected Loveliness [27].

Carnation — Antipathy; Capriciousness; Disdain.

Chrysanthemum — Cheerfulness in Adversity; Optimism [39].

Clematis — Artfulness; Artifice; Ingenuity [92].

Clover — Domestic Virtue; Fertility; Think of Me [3].

Columbine — Cuckoldry; Folly.

Cornflower — Quarrel [99].

Crocus — Abuse Not; Attachment; Mirth [59].

Daffodil — Regard [43].

Dahlia — Instability; Sterility; Treachery [96].

Daisy — Gentleness; Innocence; I Share Your Sentiments [7].

Dandelion — Coquetry [80].

Dogwood — Durability; Love in Adversity.

Edelweiss — Immortality; Perseverance; Purity [32].

Endive — Frugality.

Fern — Fascination; Reverie.

Forget-me-not — True Love [51].

Foxglove — Insincerity; Treacherous Magnificence.

Fuchsia — Amiability; Taste.

Gardenia — Secret Untold Love.

Garlic — Courage; Strength.

Gentian — Loveliness [15].

Geranium — I Shall Never See Him; Melancholy; Recall [63].

Goldenrod — Precaution; Treasure.

Hawthorn — Hope.

Heather — Admiration; Beauty in Solitude; Protection.

Heliotrope — Devotion; Faithfulness [4].

Henbane — Imperfection [72].

Hepatica — Confidence.

Holly — Defense; Foresight.

Hollyhock — Ambition; Fertility; Liberality.

Honeysuckle — Affection; Devotion; Gaiety; Generosity.

Hyacinth — Game; Play; Sport.

Hydrangea — Boastfulness; Frigidity; Heartlessness.

Iris — Eloquence; Faith; Light; Message; Promise [55].

Ivy — Eternal Friendship; Fidelity; Marriage.

Jasmine — Amiability; Cheerfulness; Grace [8].

Jonquil — Desire; Violent Sympathy.

Juniper — Confidence; Ingenuity; Protection; Succor.

Larkspur — Ardent Attachment; Fickleness; Haughtiness.

Laurel — Ambition; Glory; Renown; Success [36].

Lemon — Zest.

Lilac — First Emotion of Love; Youthful Innocence [12].

Lily — Purity of Heart; Sweetness; Virginity [23].

Lily of the Valley — Humility; Return of Happiness [111].

Lotus — Eloquence; Mystery; Perfection; Purity; Truth [35].

Lupine — Imagination; Voraciousness [87].

Magnolia — Splendid Beauty; Sweetness.

Marigold — Disquietude; Grief; Jealousy; Sorrow [84].

Mignonette — Hidden Beauty; Modesty.

Mimosa — Daintiness; Sensitiveness [16].

Mistletoe — Difficulties Surmounted [64].

Morning Glory — Affectation; Departure; Farewell [91].

Moss — Charity; Maternal Love [20].

Myrtle — Heartfelt Love; Joy; Mirth [28].

Narcissus — Conceit; Egotism; Self-love [79].

Nasturtium — Conquest; Patriotism; Victory in Battle.

Nettle — Cruelty; Slander [88].

Olive — Peace; Reconciliation; Safe Travel.

Orchid — Beauty; Magnificence; Love; Refinement.

Pansy — I Think of Thee [47].

Passion Flower — Faith; Piety; Religious Superstition [40].

Peony — Bashfulness; Shame [103].

Petunia — Anger; Resentment.

Phlox — Proposal of Love; Sweet Dreams; Unanimity.

Poppy — Dreaminess; Fantastic Extravagance; Oblivion [71].

Primrose — Inconstancy; Young Love [95].

Quince — Temptation.

Rose — Charm; Grace; Love; Pride; Simplicity [19].

Rue — Disdain.

Sage — Domestic Virtue; Esteem; Health; Longevity [24].

St. Johnswort — Animosity; Superstition; Suspicion [104].

Snapdragon — Desperation; Presumption.

Sunflower — False Appearance; Haughtiness; Homage [75].

Syringa — Beauty; Love; Memory.

Thistle — Austerity; Misanthropy; Retaliation [107].

Thornapple — Deceitful Charms [60].

Tuberose — Dangerous Pleasures.

Tulip — Declaration of Love; Dreaminess; Imagination [11].

Veronica — Fidelity.

Violet — Faithfulness; Modesty; Simplicity [31].

Walnut — Intellect; Stratagem; Trickery.

Wisteria — Poetry; Youth.

Woodbine — Fraternal Love [44].

Wormwood — Absence; Bitterness; Heartache.

Xanthium — Pertinacity; Rudeness.

Zinnia — Thoughts of Absent Friends.

REFERENCER
To Flowers by Symbolic Meaning

(As before, *italics*
indicate that the particular Flower
is described in the
main text of
this work.)

Abuse Not — *Crocus* [59].
Affectation — *Amaranth; Morning Glory* [76, 91].
Afterthought — *Aster* [67].
Ambition — Hollyhock; *Laurel* [36].
Amiability — Fuchsia; *Jasmine* [8].
Anger — Petunia.
Animosity — *St. Johnswort* [104].
Arts or Artifice — *Acanthus; Clematis* [56, 92].
Attachment — *Crocus; Jasmine*; Larkspur [59, 8].
Austerity — *Thistle* [107].
Bashfulness — *Peony* [103].
Beauty — Magnolia; Orchid; Syringa.
Bravery — *Cactus* [48].
Charity — *Moss* [20].
Cheerfulness in Adversity — *Chrysanthemum* [39].
Confidence — Hepatica; Juniper.
Coquetry — *Dandelion* [80].
Cruelty — *Nettle* [88].

117

Daintiness — *Aster; Mimosa* [67, 16].

Deceitful Charms — *Thornapple* [60].

Desire — Jonquil.

Devotion — *Heliotrope* [4]; Honeysuckle.

Difficulties Surmounted — *Mistletoe* [64].

Disdain — Carnation; Rue.

Domestic Virtue — *Clover; Sage* [3, 24].

Egotism — *Narcissus* [79].

Elegance — *Aster* [67].

Eloquence — *Iris; Lotus* [55, 35].

Endurance — *Cactus* [48].

Excellence — *Camellia* [27].

Faith — *Iris; Passion Flower* [55, 40].

Faithfulness — *Heliotrope; Violet* [4, 31].

False Appearance — *Sunflower* [75].

Fantastic Extravagance — *Poppy* [71].

Farewell — *Morning Glory* [91].

Fertility — *Clover* [3]; Hollyhock.

Fidelity — Ivy; Veronica.

First Emotion of Love — *Lilac* [12].

Folly — Columbine.

Foppery — *Amaranth* [76].

Fraternal Love — *Woodbine* [44].

Gentleness — *Daisy* [7].

Glory — *Laurel* [36].

Grace — *Jasmine; Rose* [8, 19].

Grief — *Marigold* [84].

Hatred — *Basil* [100].

Haughtiness — Larkspur; *Sunflower* [75].

I Shall Never See Him — *Geranium* [63].

I Share Your Sentiments — *Daisy* [7].

I Think of Thee — *Pansy* [47].

Imagination — *Lupine; Tulip* [87, 11].

Imperfection — *Henbane* [72].

Inconstancy — *Primrose* [95].

Ingenuity — *Clematis* [92]; Juniper.

Innocence — *Daisy* [7].

Instability — *Dahlia* [96].

Intellect — Walnut.

Jealousy — *Marigold* [84].

Love — Orchid; Syringa; *Myrtle; Rose; Tulip* [28, 19, 11].

Loveliness — *Gentian* [15].

Marriage — Ivy.

Maternal Love — *Moss* [20].

Melancholy — *Geranium* [63].

Message — *Iris* [55].

Mirth — *Crocus; Myrtle* [59, 28].

Modesty — Mignonette; *Violet* [31].

Mystery — *Lotus* [35].

Oblivion — *Poppy* [71].

Optimism — *Chrysanthemum* [39].

Peace — Olive.

Perfected Loveliness — *Camellia* [27].

Perseverance — *Edelweiss; Laurel* [32, 36].

Pride — Amaryllis; *Rose* [19].

Protection — Heather; Juniper.

Purity — *Edelweiss; Lily; Lotus* [32, 23, 35].

Quarrel — *Cornflower* [99].
Regard — *Daffodil* [43].
Religious Superstition — *Passion Flower* [40].
Return of Happiness — *Lily of the Valley* [111].
Self-love — *Narcissus* [79].
Sensitiveness — *Mimosa* [16].
Shame — *Peony* [103].
Simplicity — *Rose; Violet* [19, 31].
Slander — *Nettle* [88].
Sterility — *Dahlia* [96].
Success — *Laurel* [36].
Suspicion — *St. Johnswort* [104].
Sweetness — *Lily* [23]; Magnolia.
Temptation — *Apple* [83]; Quince.
Think of Me — *Clover* [3].
Thoughts of Absent Friends — Zinnia.
True Love — *Forget-me-not* [51].
Truth — *Lotus* [35].
Variety — *Aster* [67].
Virginity — *Lily* [23].
Voraciousness — *Lupine* [87].
Warmth — *Cactus* [48].
Youthful Innocence — *Lilac* [12].
Young Love — *Primrose* [95].
Zest — Lemon.